A Faith-Based Story to Help Children Process Grief and Loss

My Tower is Tumbling!

Written by Marci Renée — Illustrated by Layken Davey

Based on The Grief Tower by Lauren Wells

Copyright © 2023 by Marci Renée

All rights reserved. Published by The Cultural Story-Weaver.

No part of this publication may be reproduced in whole or in part, or stored in a retrieval system, or transmitted in any form or by any means, electronic, mechanical, photocopying, recording, or otherwise, without written permission of the publisher. For information regarding permission, contact The Cultural Story-Weaver at www.culturalstoryweaver.com.

ISBN: 978-1-956242-16-4

I dedicate this book to my four boys and to all the other Third Culture Kids (TCKs) in the world, along with their parents. Your life of adventure has left its marks on you. Take time to remember the good times and the hard times. They are all part of your story and what makes you YOU!

Get Your FREE Coloring Book Here!

www.culturalstoryweaver.com

Dear Parents,

Before reading this book with your children, please read this personal note.

I have written this story for all children, because everyone deals with grief and loss. However, Third Culture Kids (TCKs)—growing up across borders, languages, and cultures—have some unique challenges.

Twenty-five years ago, I didn't know what a TCK was. That's when I gave birth to my first son. I would later go on to have three more boys over the next fifteen years. Yes, we have four TCKs—ranging from ages 25 to 10!

Even though I didn't know what a TCK was back then, I knew that their lives were wonderful and exciting—full of amazing stories, experiences, people, and places. However, it didn't take me long to realize that my four boys would also walk through some deep and heartbreaking valleys of pain and loss in their unique TCK journeys.

I would watch my children face the loss of everything familiar, overbearing language and cultural barriers, scary situations of terrorism, having no friends, leaving behind too many friends, overnight evacuations due to security concerns, violent uprooting, losing favorite possessions, too many hard goodbyes, no opportunities for any goodbyes, ugly work and team conflict (their parents'), rapid transitions into different educational systems, turning their backs on pets that couldn't cross borders, distant relationships with extended family, boarding schools in faraway lands . . . the list goes on and on and on . . .

In all of our family's difficult and rushed moments of loss and transition, we never stopped to process our grief and pain. We didn't have time. We didn't have resources. We didn't know how. As a mother, I didn't know how to deal with my own broken heart, let alone, know how to help my four boys heal theirs.

So, our family did what we had to do. We packed up our own pain and grief in our suitcase to move to that next country. We also helped our boys pack up theirs. We carried our heavy bags to the next place, never taking the time to unpack them. We didn't know how, and even if we did, it would have been too scary and too overwhelming to look at!

Eventually, at some point in our journeys, our suitcases got too full, too heavy, too painful, and too burdensome to carry. Our bags tore open, and out spilled all the brokenness of our lives—the rocks from years of accumulated tears, sadness, loneliness, pain . . .

When I read Lauren Wells' book, "Unstacking Your Grief Tower for Adult TCKs," my heart broke. I saw my own life and the lives of our four boys. We had all been carrying our tall and wobbly Grief Towers! At that moment, I wished that I would have had tools and resources to help my children process their grief early on—at a young age. It would have kept them from collecting and carrying more and more rocks into their adult years. This world needs a children's picture book to help parents walk alongside their children through their stories—the good ones and the hard ones.

That's why I wrote this book. I hope that it heals your kids' hearts, as well as your own.

—Marci Renée

Pierre traveled the world with his parents and his three brothers. Their dog, Samy, went everywhere with them.

Pierre lived in many different countries—the United States, France, Morocco, Germany, Senegal, England, Holland, and Spain.

Pierre liked to explore new places, learn foreign languages, and taste delicious foods.

He loved living by the ocean, riding camels in the desert, shopping at the outdoor markets, eating couscous with his hands, drinking sweet mint tea, and reading from right to left. Pierre also liked to meet interesting people and make new friends.

Those were the good things—the fun things—Pierre experienced while he lived in faraway lands. Those were the things that made him happy, made him smile, made him want to sing and dance.

But, it wasn't all good. It wasn't all easy.

There were difficult things too—the hard things—Pierre experienced while he lived in different countries. Those were the things that made Pierre sad, made him angry, made him want to scream and cry.

Every time something difficult happened to Pierre, he picked up a rock and carried it with him on his journey. Holding something in his hand helped him remember what happened. The rock helped him hold on tightly to the memory.

When he had to leave his home and school and move to another country . . . another rock.
When he could no longer hear the ocean waves from his bedroom . . . another rock.

When he left his grandparents on the other side of the world . . . another rock.

Pierre took his rocks everywhere with him.
But, they were heavy and hard to carry.
Sometimes, Pierre couldn't play or run fast.

"What are all those rocks you're carrying?" Pierre's friend asked him.

"I don't want to talk about them," he answered.

When there were no more fun sand dunes to play on . . . another rock. When his favorite pet lizard died . . . another rock.

When he had to say goodbye to his best friend . . . another rock.

Pierre took his rocks everywhere with him. But, they were heavy and hard to carry. Sometimes Pierre was tired and his arms were sore.

"Do you want me to help carry your rocks?" Pierre's father asked him one day.

"They aren't heavy. I don't need help," he answered.

No more Arabic words, no more beach soccer, no more African drums . . . no more fresh bread and fried donuts from the corner bakery, no more mint tea in silver teapots, no more . . .

All along his journey, Pierre picked up more and more rocks . . .

Carefully carrying them everywhere he went, until . . .

CRASH! BOOM! BANG!

"My rocks are falling!" he screamed.

His mother and father heard the loud noise and came running.

"Do you want to talk about your rocks now?" his mother asked.

Pierre nodded.

"You've gone through a lot, and you've been collecting rocks along the way."

"Each one tells a story," Pierre's father said. "Good ones and hard ones."

"If we don't pay attention to our rocks, they start to stack up—just like your tower."

"Today, your tower got too tall and too wobbly, and it came tumbling down," Pierre's mother said.

"Now, it's time to look at each of your rocks. We'll be here with you, and God will help you too," Pierre's mother said.

"You can draw a picture of what you remember, or you can write a story about what happened. It may hurt, and you might cry, but that's okay. Looking at your rocks is hard and takes courage."

Pierre took time with his parents to talk about each of his rocks and to tell their stories. Then, they prayed together.

"God, thank you for the good things—the good stories—in Pierre's life. And, thank you for being with him in the hard things too—the hard stories. We give you each of these rocks—each of these stories—and ask that you would help Pierre to trust You and feel better."

It wasn't easy for Pierre to talk about his rocks, but it felt like God was lifting them out of his hands. Pierre felt better . . . lighter . . . freer.

"Can I keep my rocks?" Pierre asked.

"Of course!" his mother said. "Your rocks will always be important to you. You can keep them and remember their stories—the good and hard parts—whenever you want to and need to. Your rocks can help you remember what God did in your heart today."

Pierre picked up a rock. It said, "OMAR," the name of his best friend he had to leave in Morocco. He placed it on his desk and smiled.

"Mom, can I go out to play with my new friend, Jonathan? I can run fast now. I don't have to carry my heavy rocks anymore! God is carrying them for me!"

Note to Parents From Lauren Wells, author of The Grief Tower

In my book, "The Grief Tower: A Guide to Processing Grief with Third Culture Kids," I talk about the importance of unstacking the Grief Tower along the way. That is, processing the emotions and impact of the hard things that happen so that they don't sit unprocessed in our subconscious brain. So many of the challenges we see in Adult Third Culture Kids stem from unprocessed grief. The good news is that this is something we can prevent! We hope this simple story makes way for some deep "unstacking conversations" with your Third Culture Kids as they begin to unstack the "rocks" on their Grief Tower.

As your TCK opens up to you about the things that felt hard, it will be easy to respond with responses that unintentionally halt the conversation. These well intentioned responses often communicate that the "rock" wasn't that significant, defend the good reasons or intentions around the difficult experience, compare the experience to others who have had it worse, or correct inaccurate facts when they're trying to express their feelings. While there may be opportunity for clarifying conversations later, these "rocks" are only processed in spaces where the child feels heard and understood. At <u>TCK Training</u>, we teach to respond using the Safe Space Responses: "Acknowledge, Affirm, Comfort, and Be Curious."

Acknowledge that you're grateful your child shared their emotions/perspective/experience with you, affirm that the emotions they felt are valid and normal, comfort through connection, and gently ask questions using the following conversation starters.

Conversation Starters—Adapt to the Child's Age

- Use rocks or toy blocks to talk about each loss or difficult experience.
- How did you feel when that happened? (See the "Feeling Chart.")
- What made that feel so [insert their emotion word]?
- What was that like for you?
- What did [insert their emotion word] feel like in your body?
- Can you help me see that part of the story from your eyes, your point of view? Encourage younger children to draw a picture or use objects or toys (blocks, Legos) to help tell the story.
- Did that make you think or believe something about yourself or others? (ex. It's not safe to make friends because they always leave.)
- Do you do anything differently because that happened? (ex. I play with friends, but I don't want to have a best friend.)
- Did it make you think or believe anything about God?
- Is that something that will be helpful to keep believing or doing?
- Share a strength or character trait in your child that is connected to the "rock." (ex. Navigating that new school and all of its new rules required a lot of problem solving! You are really a great problem solver.)

Please note—if your child has experienced significant grief and loss, it may be helpful to find someone to walk alongside you and your child. TCKTraining (www.tcktraining.com) offers professional services for TCKs and their families.

Guided Prayer—By Lauren Wells, author of The Grief Tower

As your TCK opens up about the "rocks" on their Grief Tower, it invites an opportunity for you to usher them into the loving presence of God who is with us through the hard things. One wonderful way to do this is through guided prayer. Using the following prompts, pray with your child and allow at least a minute of silence between each prompt for them to hear from God. As they pray and listen, pray that God will give you wisdom and insight as you walk through these conversations with your TCK. Pray that their heart will be open to what God has to say to them.

God, we come before You with this hurt that [child's name] experienced. You know that he/she felt [list emotions]. Thank You that You are a God who comforts us.

God, as we sit here and remember this [event, experience, story], would You show [child's name] where You were when that was happening?

Ask your TCK to picture the event/experience/story and to ask God to show him/her where He was during that time.

Pause and sit in silence asking God to reveal where He was in that experience.

Thank You that You are good and that You love us. Thank You that You promise to work even the hard things like this out for the good of those who love You.

Ask your TCK if there are any questions that he/she wants to ask God about that "rock."

Pause and sit in silence, asking God to respond.

Thank You that You see the big picture even when we don't.

God, please show [child's name] Your comfort. Thank You that we can bring our difficult feelings to You and that You speak love and comfort over us. Thank You for Your lovingkindness.

Amen.

Interactive Activities for Parents and Teachers—By Marci Renée

1. Use a globe or the map on the following pages to help your child locate where he lives in the world. Then, help your child locate and identify each country where Pierre lived and its color—the United States, France, Morocco, Germany, Senegal, England, Holland, and Spain. Have him say or write the name of the countries in the "color key" in the bottom, left-hand corner.

2. Help your child reflect on his or her own life—tell his or her "rock stories."
—Where were you born? Where have you traveled or lived in the world? What colors would describe those countries? Find them on the map and color them.
—What are some of the good things—favorite objects/foods/people/experiences—from the countries where you have lived and traveled? Draw and color them on the map.
—What are some of the hard things you experienced in the countries where you lived and traveled—goodbyes, objects, activities, people you left behind, etc.? Draw and color them on the map, or draw and color rocks on those places.

3. Visit the "Kids" section at https://culturalstoryweaver.com/kids/ for coloring pages and cultural stories for kids and adults. Sign up for "Let's Weave Cultures News"! Sign up your TCK to be "Pen Pals With Pierre." Email him at theculturalstoryweaver@culturalstoryweaver.com

4. Read other TCK Books: "The Boy Who Weaves the World," "The Boy of Many Colors," "The Girl of Many Colors." https://culturalstoryweaver.com/books/

FEELING CHART

AFRAID	SAD	WORRIED	HAPPY
ASHAMED	DISTRACTED	EMBARRASSED	NERVOUS

CONFIDENT	FRUSTRATED	GUILTY	LONELY
EXHAUSTED	SURPRISED	SHY	CONFUSED
PROUD	SHOCKED	ANGRY	OVERWHELMED

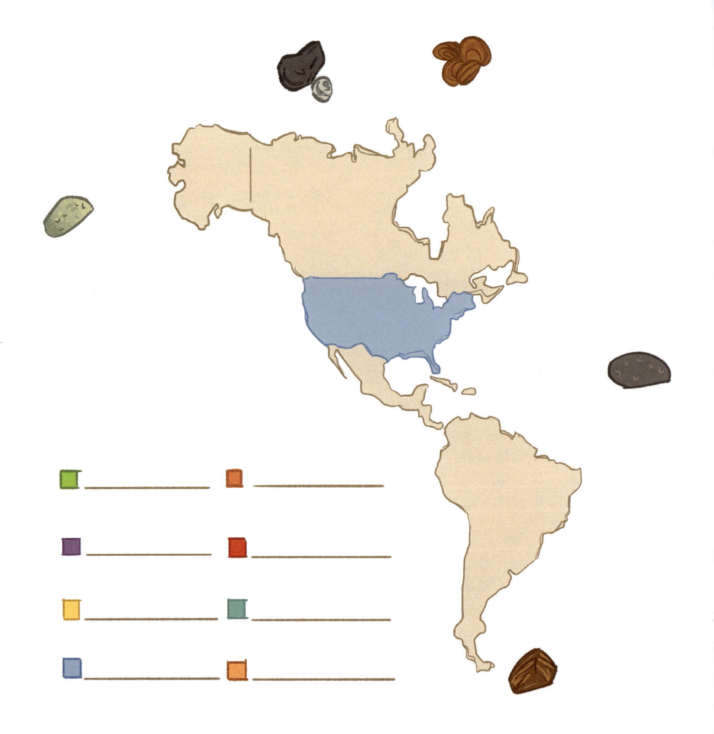

Marci Renée, along with her French husband, four boys, and dog, Samy, is a global nomad, who has traveled to more than thirty countries and has lived overseas in the United States, France, Morocco, and Spain. She loves to travel, speak foreign languages, experience different cultures, eat ethnic foods, meet people from faraway lands, and of course, tell stories. She is the published author of five children's books and four creative non-fiction memoirs. Visit her at www.culturalstoryweaver.com

Layken Davey was born in South Africa and grew up in Morocco. She loves stories, from anywhere and everywhere, and drawing characters and animals—especially horses. Layken is the illustrator of Marci's other children's picture books. Visit her at www.instagram.com/laykendavey/

Get Your FREE Coloring Book Here!

Discover Marci Renée's other children's books . . .
The Boy Who Weaves the World
The Boy of Many Colors
The Girl of Many Colors
Mommy, What's a Safe House?

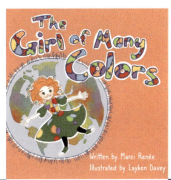
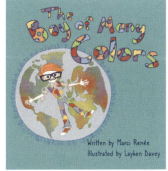
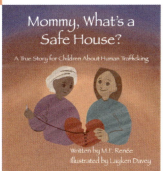

Find all her books at www.culturalstoryweaver.com/books/

Made in the USA
Middletown, DE
21 July 2023